BASS

ESSENTIAL ELEMENTS
FOR JAZZ ENSEMBLE
Book 2

A COMPREHENSIVE METHOD FOR JAZZ STYLE AND IMPROVISATION

By MIKE STEINEL

Managing Editor:
MICHAEL SWEENEY

THREE BASIC SECTIONS

I. Daily Drills, Warm-ups, and Workouts

II. Improvisation Lessons

III. Performance Spotlights (Repertoire)

This book is the second in a series and is designed for developing musicians and ensembles. The first book: *Essential Elements for Jazz Ensemble* is a comprehensive introduction to the jazz style, theory, improvisation and history. The exercises and compositions in this book can be played by a full jazz ensemble, combo, or individually with the recordings. The nine compositions for full band cover a variety of styles, tempos, and keys, and include Demonstration Solos for study and reference.

The recordings are available as a free download. Visit www.halleonard.com/mylibrary and use the code printed below to access your mp3s.

We hope you find this book helpful, and always remember…have fun playing jazz.

To access audio visit:
www.halleonard.com/mylibrary
Enter Code
J2BA-5443-7428-5976

ISBN 978-1-4950-7911-5
Copyright © 2019 by HAL LEONARD LLC
International Copyright Secured   All Rights Reserved

7777 W. BLUEMOUND RD. P.O. BOX 13819 MILWAUKEE, WI 53213

THE BASICS OF JAZZ STYLE
Review from *Essential Elements for Jazz Ensemble* (Book 1)

Jazz Articulation Review

These are the four basic articulations in jazz and the related scat syllables for each. "Doo", "Bah", "Dit" and "Dot" can be used to remind us (aurally) of the sound. However, these are not necessarily how we will articulate on the individual instruments.

Tenuto (full value) — Doo
Staccato (short, unaccented) — Dit
Long Accent (full value, accented) — Bah
Roof Top Accent (short, accented) — Dot

Attacks and Releases

In traditional music you use a "Tah" articulation to begin a note and taper the note at the end.

Tah

Doo - - it

In jazz it is common to use a "Doo" attack (soft and legato) to begin a note. It is also common to end the note with the tongue. This "tongue-stop" gives the music a rhythmic feeling.

Accenting "2 and 4"

For most traditional music the important beats in 4/4 time are 1 and 3. In jazz, however, the emphasis is usually on beats 2 and 4. Emphasizing "2 and 4" gives the music a jazz feeling.

Traditional

Jazz

Quarter Notes

In swing style quarter notes are usually played detached. In Latin or Rock they may be played with a variety of articulations but are often played full value.

Swing 8th Notes Sound Different Than They Look

In swing the 2nd 8th note of each beat is actually played like the last third of a triplet, and slightly accented. 8th notes in swing style are usually played legato.

Doo Bah Doo Bah Doo Bah Doo Bah   Doo Bah Doo Bah Doo Bah Doo Bah

8ths in Latin and Rock (Straight 8th Music)

8th Notes in Latin or Rock are played evenly and the articulations are often quite different than in swing style.

Dit Dit Dot Dit Dit Dit Dot Dit   Dit Dit Dot Dit Dit Dit Dot Dit

Jazz Ornamentation and Expression

There are many ornaments and articulations which are associated with jazz and necessary to achieve a characteristic jazz feeling. These are the most common:

Bend: Start the note on pitch, lower it momentarily, then return to original pitch.

Fall: At the end of the note let the pitch fall off. Falls may be executed with the embouchure or the fingers or a combination of both. Falls can be short or long.

Scoop: Slide into the note from below pitch. Scoops can be executed with the embouchure or the fingers or a combination of both.

Doit: Slide the pitch upwards at the end of the note.

Plop: Slide down to a note from above slightly before the note is to be played. Plops can be short or long.

Glissando: Slide from one note to the next smoothly. Glissandos may be executed with the embouchure or the fingers or a combination of both.

Flip Often called a turn, the flip is executed by quickly playing a note above the original note (usually a step or half step), returning to the original note and then proceeding to the next written note.

BASIC JAZZ THEORY AND IMPROVISATION
Review from *Essential Elements for Jazz Ensemble* (Book 1)

Chord and Scale Review

Chord Type	Chord Symbol	Related Scale or Mode for Improvisation
Major Seventh	BbMA7	Bb Major Scale
Dominant Seventh	Bb7	Bb Mixolydian Mode — Note: the Blues Scale can be used with Dominant Seventh Chords, Minor Seventh Chords, and the entire Blues Progression — Bb Blues Scale
Minor Seventh	Bbmi7	Bb Dorian Mode — Bb Blues Scale

The Dominant Seventh Chord is a "jazzy" chord
Because of its flattened seventh (often called a "blue note") the **Dominant Seventh Chord** has a very "jazzy" or "bluesy" sound.

The Blues Progression
The harmony of a jazz song is called the chord progression. The most common chord progression in jazz is the blues. Usually the blues is a twelve-bar repeated pattern using three **Dominant Seventh Chords**. The roots (bottom notes) of these three chords are usually the first, fourth, and fifth notes of the key of the blues.

Common Blues Progression in B♭ using Dominant Chords and Mixolydian Modes

Common Blues Progression in F using Dominant Chords and Mixolydian Modes

Two Common Blues Scales (Minor and Major)
Minor and Major Blues Scales in B♭

Minor and Major Blues Scales in F

DAILY DRILLS, WARM-UPS AND WORKOUTS

1. BASIC SCALE AND STYLE WORKOUT #1 – Major Scale

2. BASIC SCALE AND STYLE WORKOUT #2 – Major Scale

3. BASIC SCALE AND STYLE WORKOUT #3 – Mixolydian Mode

4. BASIC SCALE AND STYLE WORKOUT #4 – Mixolydian Mode

5. BASIC SCALE AND STYLE WORKOUT #5 – Dorian Mode

6. BASIC SCALE AND STYLE WORKOUT #6 – Harmonic Minor

RHYTHM WORKOUTS FOR READING AND STYLE

All exercises are played in a Swing style.

7. HALF MEASURE RHYTHMS

8. COMBINING COMMON RHYTHMS #1

9. COMBINING COMMON RHYTHMS #2

10. COMBINING COMMON RHYTHMS #3

11. COMBINING COMMON RHYTHMS #4

12. COMBINING COMMON RHYTHMS #5

13. COMBINING COMMON RHYTHMS #6 – Adding Ties

RHYTHM WORKOUTS FOR READING AND STYLE (STRAIGHT 8THS)

14. COMBINING COMMON RHYTHMS #7

15. COMBINING COMMON RHYTHMS #8

16. SCALE AND RHYTHM WORKOUT

17. MELODY AND RHYTHM WORKOUT #1

18. MELODY AND RHYTHM WORKOUT #2

JAZZ EXPRESSION WORKOUTS

All exercises are played in a Swing style.

19. STYLE CONCEPT – Syllables for Jazz Expression

20. SCOOPS, FALLS, BENDS AND DOITS

21. PLOPS, GLISSANDI AND FLIPS

22. MELODY AND EXPRESSION WORKOUT #1

23. MELODY AND RHYTHM WORKOUT #2

24. NEW CONCEPT: GHOSTED NOTES

Often single notes in jazz lines are played very softly and without accent. These notes can be notated with an "x" instead of a notehead. Lines with ghosted 8th notes are usually played legato.

25. JAZZ EXPRESSION ETUDE

MAJOR SCALES BY NUMBERS

33. MAJOR SCALE WORKOUT

34. MAJOR SCALE BY THE NUMBERS #1 *Play using only the numbers.*

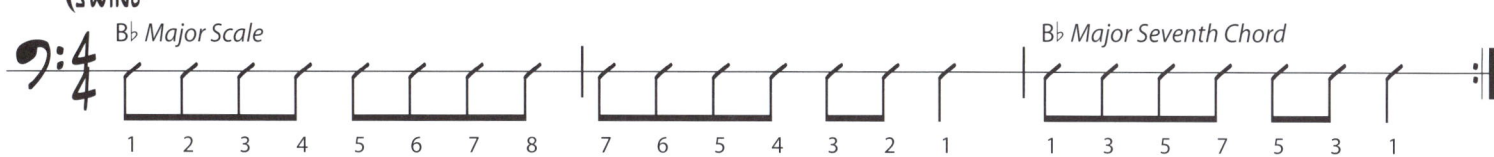

35. MAJOR SCALE BY THE NUMBERS #2

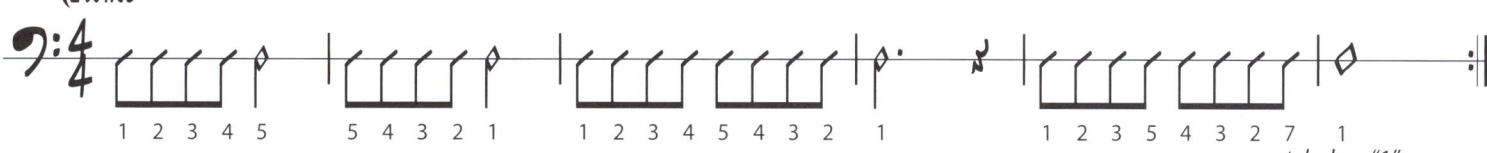

▲ *below "1"*

36. MAJOR SCALE BY THE NUMBERS #3

37. MAJOR SCALE BY THE NUMBERS #4

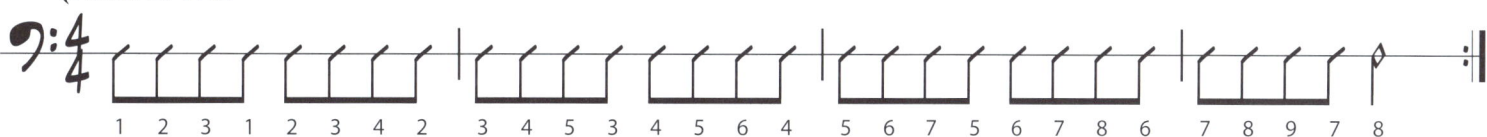

38. MAJOR SCALE BY THE NUMBERS #5

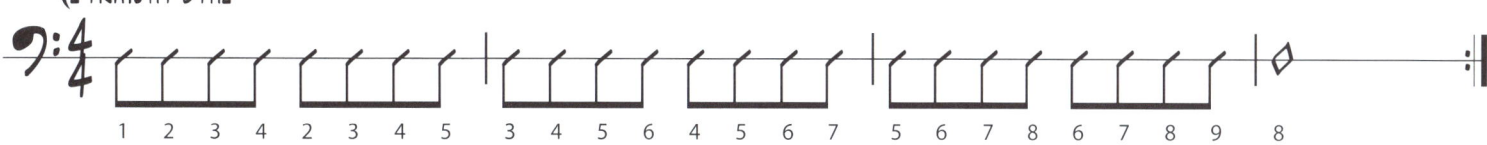

39. MAJOR SCALE BY THE NUMBERS #6

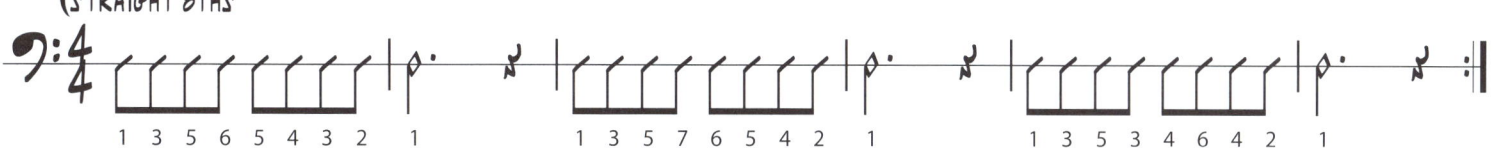

Additional Workouts – Repeat the scale patterns in exercises 34 through 39 using these common keys.

MIXOLYDIAN MODE BY NUMBERS

40. MIXOLYDIAN WORKOUT

41. MIXOLYDIAN BY THE NUMBERS #1 *Play using the numbers.*
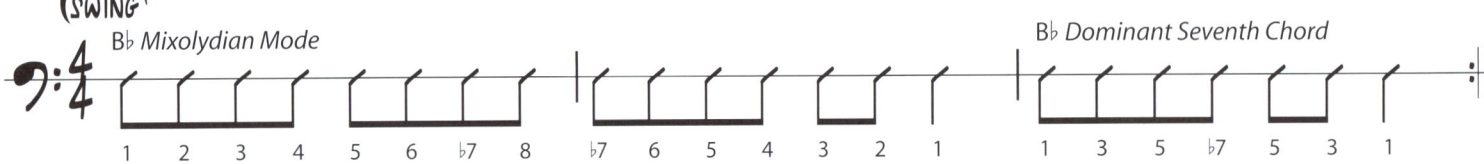

42. MIXOLYDIAN BY THE NUMBERS #2
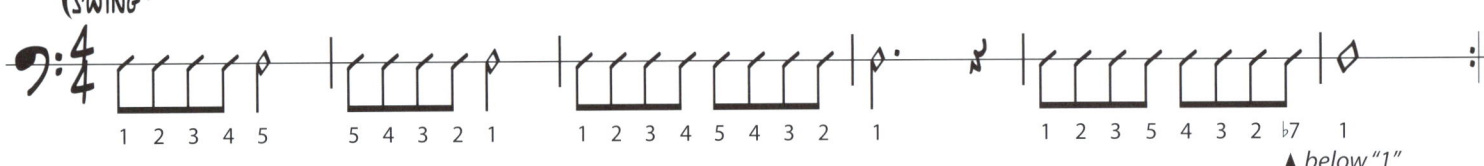

43. MIXOLYDIAN BY THE NUMBERS #3
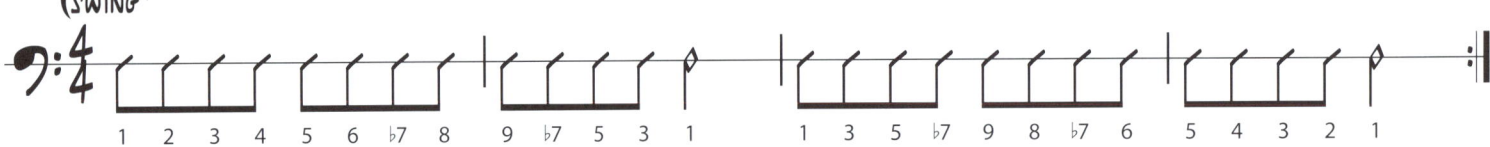

44. MIXOLYDIAN BY THE NUMBERS #4
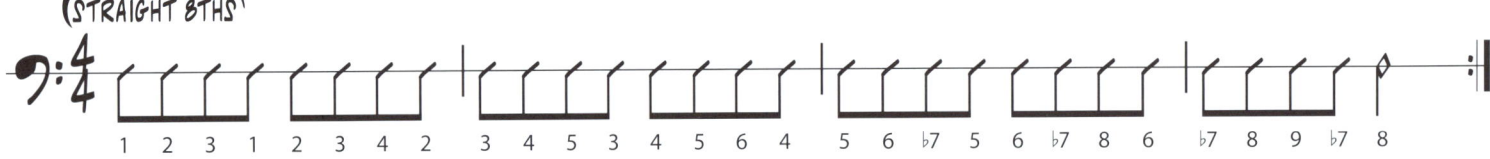

45. MIXOLYDIAN BY THE NUMBERS #5
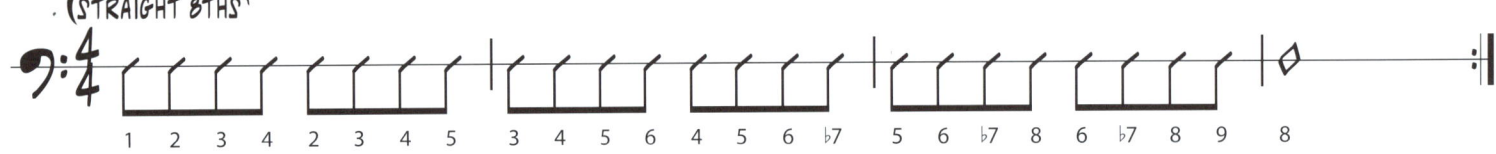

46. MIXOLYDIAN BY THE NUMBERS #6
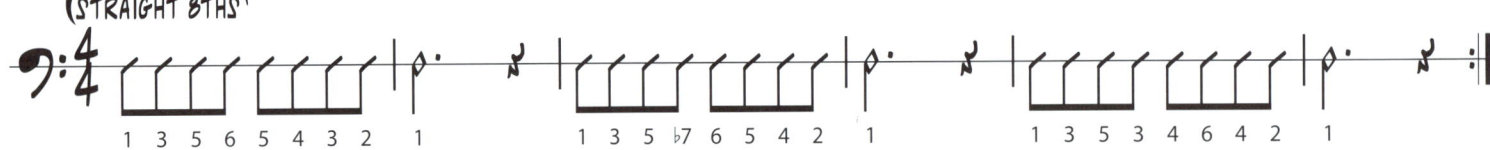

Additional Workouts – Repeat the scale patterns in exercises 40 through 46 using these common Mixolydian modes.

DORIAN MODE BY NUMBERS

47. DORIAN WORKOUT

48. DORIAN BY THE NUMBERS #1 *Play using the numbers.*
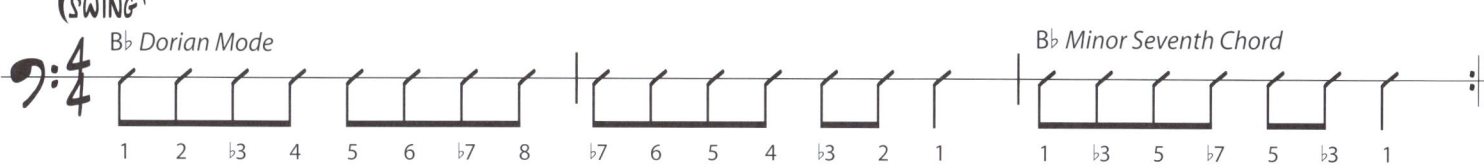

49. DORIAN BY THE NUMBERS #2
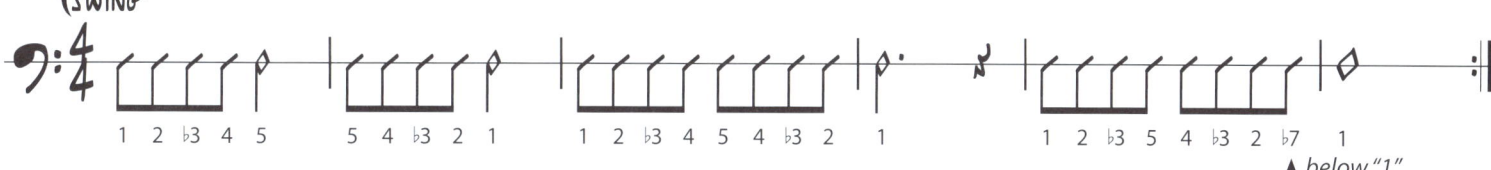

50. DORIAN BY THE NUMBERS #3
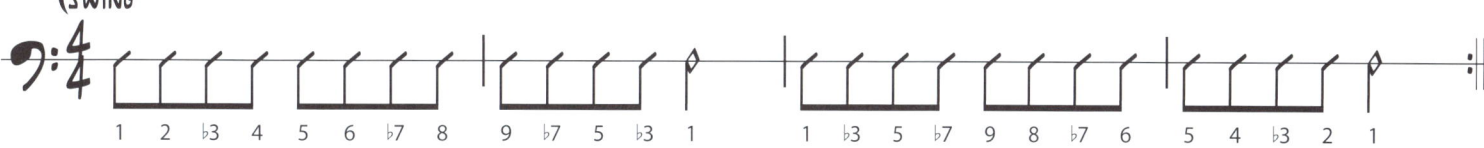

51. DORIAN BY THE NUMBERS #4
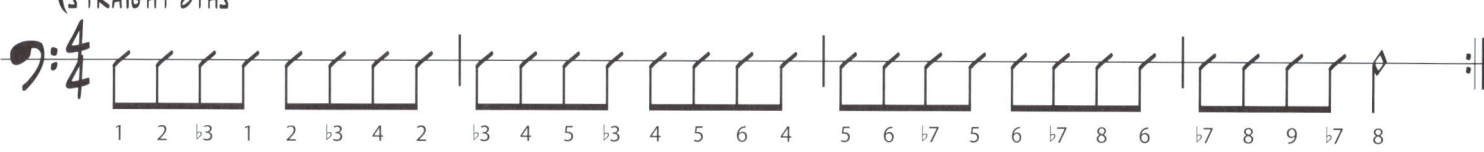

52. DORIAN BY THE NUMBERS #5
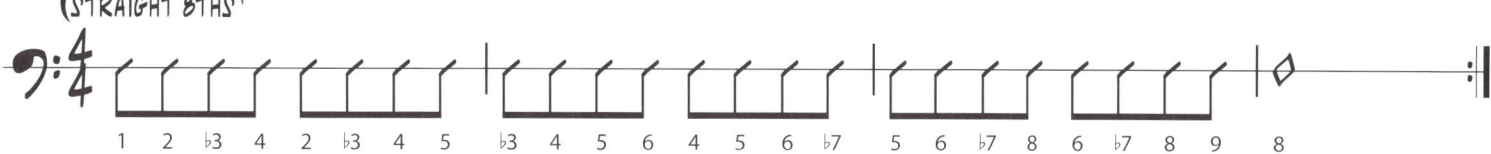

53. DORIAN BY THE NUMBERS #6

Additional Workouts – Repeat the scale patterns in exercises 47 through 53 using these common Dorian modes.

SCALE WORKOUTS – PENTATONIC AND BLUES SCALES IN CONCERT B♭

54. SCALE WORKOUT #1 – Minor Pentatonic

55. SCALE WORKOUT #2 – Minor Pentatonic

56. SCALE WORKOUT #3 – Minor Blues

57. SCALE WORKOUT #4 – Minor Blues

58. SCALE WORKOUT #5 – Major Blues

59. SCALE WORKOUT #6 – Major Blues

SCALE WORKOUTS – PENTATONIC AND BLUES SCALES IN CONCERT F

60. SCALE WORKOUT #1 – Minor Pentatonic

61. SCALE WORKOUT #2 – Minor Pentatonic

62. SCALE WORKOUT #3 – Minor Blues

63. SCALE WORKOUT #4 – Minor Blues

64. SCALE WORKOUT #5 – Major Blues

65. SCALE WORKOUT #6 – Major Blues

ADVANCED WORKOUTS – PENTATONIC AND BLUES SCALES IN CONCERT B♭

66. ADVANCED WORKOUT #1 – Minor Pentatonic

67. ADVANCED WORKOUT #2 – Minor Pentatonic

68. ADVANCED WORKOUT #3 – Minor Blues

69. ADVANCED WORKOUT #4 – Major Blues

70. ADVANCED WORKOUT #5 – Blues Riffs

71. ADVANCED WORKOUT #6 – Blues Riffs

ADVANCED WORKOUTS – PENTATONIC AND BLUES SCALES IN CONCERT F

72. ADVANCED WORKOUT #1 – Minor Pentatonic

73. ADVANCED WORKOUT #2 – Minor Pentatonic

74. ADVANCED WORKOUT #3 – Minor Blues

75. ADVANCED WORKOUT #4 – Major Blues

76. ADVANCED WORKOUT #5 – Blues Riffs

77. ADVANCED WORKOUT #6 – Blues Riffs

PERFORMANCE SPOTLIGHT *The Saints Are Swingin' Low*

New Orleans, generally recognized as the birthplace of jazz, was a major economic and cultural center in the southern United States at the beginning of the 20th century. The very first jazz ensembles were the brass bands that played in a ragtime style. Famous musicians from New Orleans include:

Buddy Bolden	Sidney Bechet	Fats Domino	Dr. John
Louis Armstrong	Wynton Marsalis	Professor Longhair	The Dirty Dozen Brass Band
Jelly Roll Morton	Harry Connick Jr.	Louis Prima	Terence Blanchard

Rhythmic Concept – *"Second Line Rhythmic Feel"* is a style of drumming that originated in New Orleans. The 8th notes in a *"Second Line"* feel are played between what would be straight 8ths and regular triplet-oriented swing 8th notes.

92. STRAIGHT, SWING AND SECOND LINE 8TH NOTES

Rhythmic Concept – *Tresillo Rhythm* is a three note rhythm which is very common in New Orleans music and early Rock 'n' Roll.

93. WORKOUT FOR RHYTHMIC FEEL AND GROOVE

94. MELODY WORKOUT FOR "SAINTS"

95. MELODY WORKOUT FOR "SWING LOW"

96. THE SAINTS ARE SWINGIN' LOW – Full Band Arrangement

97. DEMONSTRATION SOLO FOR "THE SAINTS ARE SWINGIN' LOW"

98. PRACTICE TRACK FOR "THE SAINTS ARE SWINGIN' LOW" – mm. 26-42 (3 choruses)

LESSON #3 Blues Riffs

Improvisation Concept – *Riffs are short melodies that are common parts of jazz solos often using notes of the blues scales (minor and major). Blues songs and solos often use three identical four-bar riffs.*

All Lesson #3 exercises are played in a Swing style.

99. BLUES RIFF #1 *Blues Riff played 3 times over a twelve-bar blues.*

100. BLUES RIFF #2

Theory Concept – *Often the 3rd of the key is flatted to fit better with the IV chord.*

101. "ROVING THIRD" RIFF #1

▲ This note is flatted to fit the chord.

102. "ROVING THIRD" RIFF #2

▲ This note is flatted to fit the chord.

103. "ROVING THIRD" RIFF #3

▲ 3rd is flatted to fit the chord.

104. "ROVING THIRD" RIFF #4

▼ 3rd is flattened to fit the chord.

LESSON #4 *Call and Response*

Improvisation Concept – *Call and Response* is a traditional way of playing or singing melodies common in African American Church music of the 19th and 20th centuries.

All Lesson #4 exercises are played in a Swing style.

Improvisation Concept – *Improvising using Short Call and Response Riffs. Often songs and solos use two-bar phrases in a "Call and Response" style. The responses usually start in bars 3, 7, and 11 and are similar or identical.*

PERFORMANCE SPOTLIGHT *Vine Street Ruckus*

In the 1930s **Kansas City** was home to some of the greatest musicians in jazz. Bands led by Count Basie and Jay McShann played a swing style of music that drew heavily on the blues tradition of "Call and Response." Important musicians from or associated with Kansas City Jazz:

Charlie Parker	Claude Williams	Buck Clayton	Hot Lips Page	Count Basie
Bobby Watson	Coleman Hawkins	Lester Young	Jay McShann	Pat Metheny
Bob Brookmeyer	Ben Webster	Andy Kirk	Mary Lou Williams	Jimmy Rushing
Walter Page	Jimmy Lunceford	Hershel Evans	Big Joe Turner	Bennie Moten

110. MELODY WORKOUT #1 – Main Riff

111. MELODY WORKOUT #2 – Response Riff

112. "VINE STREET RUCKUS" – Full Band Arrangement

113. DEMONSTRATION SOLO FOR "VINE STREET RUCKUS"

114. PRACTICE TRACK FOR "VINE STREET RUCKUS" – mm. 45-56 (4 choruses)

LESSON #6 Composite Blues Scale

Theory Concept – The Composite Blues Scale *is formed by combining the Minor Blues Scale and the Major Blues Scale. The Composite Blues Scale has 9 different notes.*

Bb Minor Blues Scale   Bb Major Blues Scale   Bb Composite Blues Scale

All Lesson #6 exercises are played with Straight 8ths.

122. THEORY WORKOUT *Compare the Minor, Major, and Composite Blues Scales.*

123. COMPOSITE BLUES SCALE WORKOUT #1

124. COMPOSITE BLUES SCALE WORKOUT #2

125. COMPOSITE BLUES SCALE WORKOUT #3

PERFORMANCE SPOTLIGHT *Beale Street Barbeque*

On December 15, 1977, **Beale Street** (in Memphis, TN) was officially declared the "Home of the Blues" by an act of the U.S. Congress. Memphis was an important music center throughout the 20th century and Memphis musicians influenced all types of American music including jazz, blues, soul, gospel and Rock 'n' Roll. Famous musicians associated with Memphis include:

Elvis Presley	Howlin' Wolf	Booker T. Jones	Memphis Minnie	W.C. Handy
Aretha Franklin	B.B. King	Isaac Hayes	Booker Little	George Coleman

126. MELODY WORKOUT

127. RHYTHM WORKOUT – Bass Vamp

128. "BEALE STREET BARBEQUE" – Full Band Arrangement

129. DEMONSTRATION SOLO FOR "BEALE STREET BARBEQUE"

130. PRACTICE TRACK FOR "BEALE STREET BARBEQUE" – mm. 35-42 (6 choruses)

LESSON #7 *Triplets in Swing and Dorian Vamp*

Improvisation Concept – *Triplets are very important in making jazz swing. Often the underlying rhythmic subdivision in swing is the triplet. Not all music in a swing feel is interpreted as a strict triplet. Generally at faster tempos the 8ths are more equal in value.*

All Lesson #7 exercises are played in a Swing style.

131. TRIPLET WORKOUT #1
(Swing 8ths)

132. TRIPLET WORKOUT #2

Dit Dot Dit Doo Doo Bah Dit Dot Dit Doo Doo Bah Dit Doo Doo Bah Dit Dot Dit Doo Doo Bah Dit Dot

Dit Doo Doo Bah Dit Doo Doo Bah Dit Doo Doo Bah Dit Doo Doo Bah Dit Doo Bah Dit Dot Dit Doo Bah Dit Dot

133. TRIPLET WORKOUT #3

Dit Dot Doo Bah Dot Dit Dot Doo Bah Dot Doo Bah Dot Doo Bah Dot Doo Bah Dot Doo Bah Dot

Doo Bah Doo Doo Bah Dit Doo Bah Doo Doo Bah Dit Doo Dot Doo Dot Doo Bah Dot Doo Dot Doo Dot Doo Bah Dot

Theory Review – The Major Scale has seven modes. *Each mode is built on a different note of the scale. Each mode has a unique sound, unique name, and works well with a specific chord type. Ionian is another name for the Major Scale.*

134. SEVEN MODES OF THE MAJOR SCALE (Concert B♭)   *Play each of the modes while listening to the related chords.*

B♭MA7 B♭ Ionian Mode   CMI7 C Dorian Mode   DMI7 D Phrygian Mode   E♭MA7 E♭ Lydian Mode

F7 F Mixolydian Mode   GMI7 G Aeolian Mode   AMI7(♭5) A Locrian Mode   B♭MA7

Theory Concept – Modal Vamp Using The Dorian Mode (2nd Mode). *Many jazz songs are written using the Dorian Mode. Interesting vamps can be made by building a chord on each note of the mode.*

135. DORIAN WORKOUT   *Play the mode then pick any note in the chords.*

C Dorian Mode   Chords built on each note of the C Dorian Mode

LESSON #8   *Dorian Vamp and Minor Pentatonic Scale*

136. DORIAN VAMP   *Listen the first time then play any note in the chords on the repeat.*

137. DORIAN WORKOUT WITH TRIPLETS*

138. DORIAN MODE – 9th, 6th, and 11th*

Theory Review – Pentatonic Scales have five notes. There are two basic pentatonic scales: Major Pentatonic and Minor Pentatonic. The Minor Pentatonic sounds very similar to the Dorian Mode.

139. DORIAN/MINOR PENTATONIC

140. MINOR PENTATONIC WORKOUT WITH TRIPLETS*

*Play vamp from Ex. 136 if play-along track is not being used.

PERFORMANCE SPOTLIGHT *Windy City*

Musicians from New Orleans such as Joe "King" Oliver and Louis Armstrong brought jazz to **Chicago** in the 1920s and became important influences for the local musicians. The "Windy City" quickly became an important center for jazz music and remains so today. Some important musicians from Chicago include:

Paul Butterfield	Nat King Cole	Jack DeJohnette	Kurt Elling	Chaka Khan	Benny Goodman
Lester Bowie	Bud Freeman	Dinah Washington	Herbie Hancock	Gene Krupa	Ramsey Lewis
Chicago (The Band)	Lou Rawls	Lennie Tristano	Jimmy McPartland	Lil Hardin Armstrong	Buddy Guy

141. RHYTHM WORKOUT

142. MELODY WORKOUT

143. COUNTER MELODY WORKOUT

LESSON #9 *Bebop Scale and Double-Time Playing*

Theory Review – Adding a note between the seventh and root of the Mixolydian mode produces a Bebop Scale. This was a common sound in the Bebop era and has been used in many jazz styles.

All Lesson #9 exercises are played with Straight 8ths.

147. MIXOLYDIAN MODE/BEBOP SCALE

148. MIXOLYDIAN MODE/BEBOP SCALE WORKOUT

Theory Concept – The **"Bebop Lick"** uses four 8th notes and three pitches. One of the notes is repeated.

149. BEBOP LICK WORKOUT #1

150. BEBOP LICK WORKOUT #2

Improvisation Concept – At times the Bebop lick is played on a dissonant note to add tension to the music.

151. BEBOP LICK WORKOUT #3

Rhythmic Concept – *Double Time* (or *"Doubling Up"*) is often played with 16th note rhythms. These will sound the same as 8th note rhythms at a faster tempo but with a "half time feel."

152. DOUBLE-TIME WORKOUT #1

153. DOUBLE-TIME WORKOUT #2

154. DOUBLE-TIME WORKOUT #3
F Mixolydian Bebop

LESSON #10 The Ten-Note Bebop Scale

Improvisation Concept – *Sometimes chromatic notes are added to the basic eight-note Bebop Scales.*

All Lesson #10 exercises are played with Straight 8ths.

155. TEN-NOTE MIXOLYDIAN BEBOP SCALE
Ten-Note F Mixolydian Scale

Added Notes

156. TEN-NOTE MIXOLYDIAN BEBOP SCALE WORKOUT #1

157. TEN-NOTE MIXOLYDIAN BEBOP SCALE WORKOUT #2

158. ADDING CHROMATIC NOTES *Often the ♭3 is placed on a downbeat to create a bluesy effect.*

PERFORMANCE SPOTLIGHT *Baytown Boogaloo*

Tower Of Power has been one of the most successful jazz/rock fusion ensembles since the 1970s. Formed in Oakland, CA, their sound is a unique blend of Rhythm & Blues elements, precision horn section work, tightly constructed bass lines, and infectious drum grooves. Much of their music is played in a 16th note rock feel. "Baytown Boogaloo" is written in a *Tower of Power* style.

161. "BAYTOWN BOOGALOO" – Full Band Arrangement

162. DEMONSTRATION SOLO FOR "BAYTOWN BOOGALOO"

163. PRACTICE TRACK FOR "BAYTOWN BOOGALOO" – mm. 25-32 (4 choruses)

LESSON #11 *9th Chords and Chord Tone Soloing*

Theory Concept – *The Dominant 7th* Chord (see page 3) is the most common chord in jazz because it has a naturally "bluesy" sound. Often the 9th is added.

All Lesson #11 exercises are played in a Swing style.

164. DOMINANT 7TH AND 9TH CHORDS

165. TYPICAL PROGRESSION USING DOMINANT 9TH CHORD

Improvisation Concept – *Chord Tone Soloing*: Jazz musicians use chord tones to make interesting solo melodies.

166. CHORD TONE WORKOUT

Rhythmic Concept – *For rhythmic variety add Triplets and start on upbeats.*

167. TRIPLET ARPEGGIOS

Improvisation Concept – *For melodic variety start on notes other than the root of the chord.*

168. ARPEGGIOS STARTING ON 3

169. ARPEGGIOS STARTING ON 9

170. ARPEGGIOS STARTING ON 5

LESSON #12 *Chromatic and Passing Tones*

Improvisation Concept – *Adding chromatic ornamentation to simple arpeggios can make the chord tones more interesting and jazzy.*

All Lesson #12 exercises are played in a Swing style.

171. CHROMATIC TONE BELOW THE ROOT

172. CHROMATIC TONE BELOW THE THIRD

173. STARTING ON THE UPBEAT AND ADDING A TRIPLET

174. CHROMATIC TONE BELOW THE FIFTH

175. CHROMATIC TONE BELOW THE NINTH

Improvisation Concept – *Using passing tones between chord tones is an effective melodic device. Avoid skipping between non-chord tones: 4 and 6.*

176. ADDING 2 BETWEEN 1 AND 3

177. ADDING 6 BETWEEN 5 AND 7

178. PASSING TONE WORKOUT

PERFORMANCE SPOTLIGHT Liberty Bell Shuffle

The Declaration of Independence was ratified in **Philadelphia** on July 4, 1776. Important jazz musicians from Philadelphia include:

John Coltrane	Philly Joe Jones	Michael Brecker	Randy Brecker	Clifford Brown	Stan Getz
Billie Holiday	Jimmy McGriff	Lee Morgan	McCoy Tyner	Stanley Clarke	Kenny Barron
Pat Martino	Bobby Timmons	Red Rodney	Jimmy Garrison	Sonny Fortune	Hank Mobley
Jimmy Smith	Archie Shepp	Rashied Ali			

179. MELODY WORKOUT

180. "LIBERTY BELL SHUFFLE" – Full Band Arrangement

181. DEMONSTRATION SOLO FOR "LIBERTY BELL SHUFFLE"

182. PRACTICE TRACK FOR "LIBERTY BELL SHUFFLE" – mm. 34-41 (4 choruses)

LESSON #13 *ii–V–I in Major and Minor*

Theory Concept – Chord Function in Major and Minor. A chord can be built on each step of the major and minor scales. The chords are often labeled using Roman Numerals.

All Lesson #13 exercises are played with Straight 8ths.

183. CHORDS OF MAJOR AND RELATIVE MINOR KEYS
Relative Minor has the same notes and key signature as Major but starts on the 6th note of the Major scale.

Theory Concept – Two common chord progressions are ii-V-I in Major and ii-V-I in Minor. In B♭ Major the ii chord is Cmi7, the V chord is F7, and I is B♭MA7. In G Minor the ii chord is Ami7b5, the V chord is D7b9, and I is Gmi7. (Often the Major version includes the IV chord: ii-V-I-IV).

184. ARPEGGIOS OF ii–V–I–IV IN MAJOR AND ii–V–I IN THE RELATIVE MINOR
Listen to the chords and play the arpeggios.

Note: the ii and V chord in Minor Keys are altered. The ii has a flatted 5th and the V has a flatted 9th.

185. IMPROVISATION WORKOUT – Scales over ii–V–I–IV in Major

Improvisation Concept – Scale Bracketing – If the progression stays in one key the scale of that key can often be used as melodic material. Listen to the scale over the entire progression. Some notes may sound a bit dissonant.

186. MAJOR SCALE OVER THE ENTIRE ii–V–I–IV IN MAJOR

LESSON #14 *Scale Bracketing*

Theory Concept – Scale Bracketing with the Dorian Scale: The C Dorian mode works with Cmi7 (ii) and also F7 (V). Likewise the B♭ Major scale works with B♭ma7 (I) and also E♭ma7 (IV).

All Lesson #14 exercises are played with Straight 8ths.

187. DORIAN MODE AND MAJOR SCALE OVER ii–V–I–IV

Improvisation Concept – *Scale Bracketing in Minor:* The Minor scale works well over ii and I chord, but Harmonic Minor sounds better with V chord (it has ♭9 of the V chord).

188. MINOR SCALE AND HARMONIC MINOR SCALE OVER ii–V–I

Theory Concept – *Raising the 7th note of the Minor Scale produces the Harmonic Minor scale.*

189. IMPROVISATION WORKOUT   *Three scales for ii–V–I in Minor*

190. COMPARE THE MINOR SCALE AND THE HARMONIC MINOR SCALE

191. HARMONIC MINOR (starting on the 5th) AND MINOR SCALE OVER ii–V–I IN MINOR

PERFORMANCE SPOTLIGHT *Ipanema Dreamin'*

Ipanema is a famous beach in Rio de Janeiro, Brazil. The **Bossa Nova** is a type of Latin music which originated in Brazil and became very popular worldwide in the 1950s and 1960s. Antonio Carlos Jobim's "Girl From Ipanema" was a big pop hit for Stan Getz (tenor sax). In 1965 it won a *Grammy* for "Record of the Year". It is one of the three most often recorded songs in history. Notable musicians associated with the Bossa Nova:

Antonio Carlos Jobim	Astrud Gilberto	Joao Gilberto	Sergio Mendez
Edu Lobo	Luiz Bonfá	Roberto Menescal	Hermeto Pascoal

192. MELODY WORKOUT

193. "IPANEMA DREAMIN'" – Full Band Arrangement

194. DEMONSTRATION SOLO FOR "IPANEMA DREAMIN'"

195. PRACTICE TRACK FOR "IPANEMA DREAMIN'" – mm. 41-56 (4 choruses)

PERFORMANCE SPOTLIGHT *Skating In The Park*

The **Modern Jazz Quartet** was one of the most successful small ensembles in the "modern jazz era." **Skating In Central Park** by pianist John Lewis is one of their most famous compositions. "Skating In The Park" is a tribute to that song and to New York City, the home of Central Park. New York City became the most important center for jazz music in the last half of the 20th century. Nearly all the great jazz musicians in history have performed at New York's most famous jazz clubs: The Village Vanguard, The Blue Note, the Savoy Ballroom, the Village Gate, the Five Spot, and Birdland.

Theory Concept – *Jazz played in swing style in 3/4 time can have a variety of accents.*

PERFORMANCE SPOTLIGHT *Five's A Crowd*

West Coast Jazz (often referred to as "Cool Jazz") is a style of jazz music that developed in the 1950s. West Coast Jazz was more sedate than bebop or hard bop. One of the most important recordings in this style is Dave Brubeck's *Time Out* which experimented with various time signatures. The most famous song from *Time Out* was "Take Five" by saxophonist Paul Desmond, which used the time signature of 5/4. Desmond was Brubeck's musical partner for many years. Important musicians associated with Cool Jazz or West Coast Jazz include:

Miles Davis	Gerry Mulligan	Dave Brubeck	Chet Baker	Lee Konitz
George Shearing	Shorty Rogers	Shelly Manne	Bud Shank	Art Farmer

203. RHYTHM WORKOUT

204. THEORY WORKOUT – Two Chord Vamp in Dorian
Listen, then play. Pick any note.

205. IMPROVISATION WORKOUT #1 – Using the Dorian Mode Over the Two Chord Vamp

206. IMPROVISATION WORKOUT #2 – Chord Tones
Effective solos can be built using the chord tones.

207. MELODY WORKOUT

208. "FIVE'S A CROWD" – Full Band Arrangement

209. DEMONSTRATION SOLO FOR "FIVE'S A CROWD"

210. PRACTICE TRACK FOR "FIVE'S A CROWD" – mm. 25-32 (8 choruses)